LOW CHOLESTEROL COOKBOOK

Photography by Peter Barry
Designed by Claire Leighton and
  Helen Johnson
Edited by Jillian Stewart and Kate Cranshaw

3568
© 1994 Coombe Books
This edition published 1994
for Parragon Book Service Ltd., Unit 13-17, Avonbridge Trading Estate,
Atlantic Road, Avonmouth, Bristol BS11 9QD
Printed in Hong Kong
ISBN 1-85813-568-0

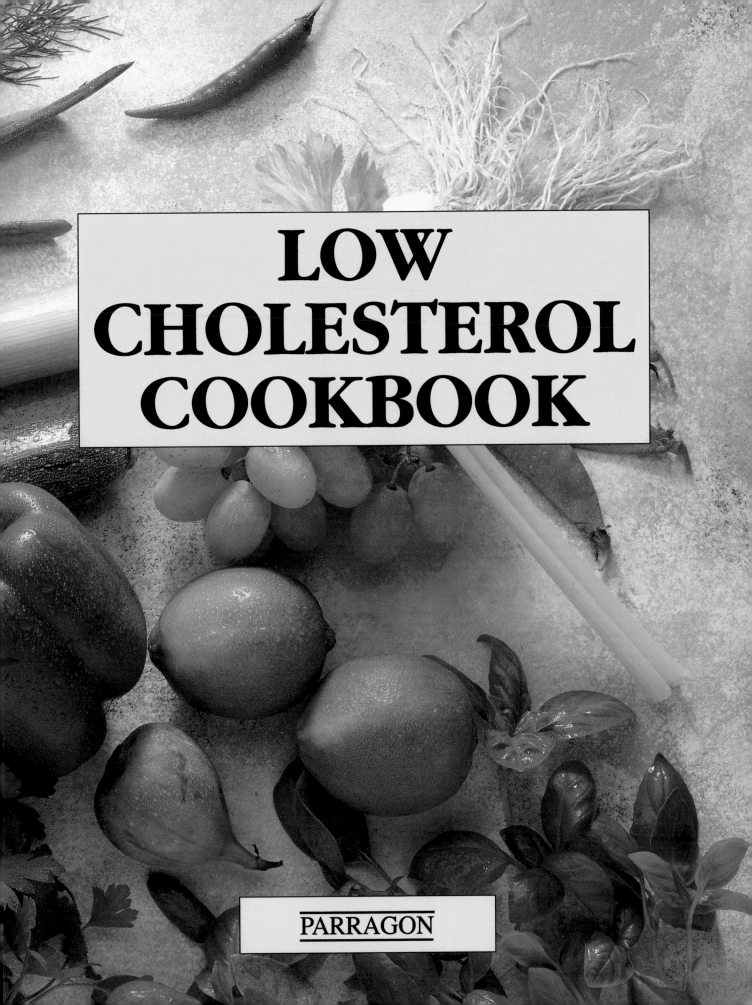

LOW
CHOLESTEROL
COOKBOOK

PARRAGON

Contents

Introduction *page 7*

Soups and Starters *page 8*

Salads and Vegetarian Meals *page 18*

Fish and Seafood *page 44*

Poultry and Meat *page 64*

Side Dishes *page 82*

Sweet Treats *page 92*

Introduction

Many of the so-called diseases of civilisation such as heart disease, cancer, high blood pressure and obesity are becoming increasingly linked with high-cholesterol diets. Cholesterol is a fat-like substance which is produced in the bodies of all animals, including humans and all animal foods therefore contain some cholesterol. Cholesterol is an important body constituent required for normal day-to-day functioning and we do need a certain amount, although the body produces its own cholesterol and needs little help from dietary intake.

Saturated fats are thought to be responsible for raising blood cholesterol and for clogging the arteries, in particular the vital coronary arteries and it is widely believed that a diet high in saturated fats is one of the main risk factors leading to life-threatening heart disease, especially for those who have a hereditary problem and who smoke or are obese. In addition, physical inactivity and emotional stress are also thought to increase the body's own cholesterol levels.

There is still much debate within medical and dietary circles concerning cholesterol, but current thinking dictates the following main guidelines regarding fats. Firstly, and most importantly, cut right down on saturated fats. The main sources in the diet are are offal, fatty meats, lard, egg yolk, butter, whole milk, high-fat cheeses, ice-cream and coconut and palm oil. Secondly, substitute these saturated fats with the benign monounsaturates and the polyunsaturates which do not raise cholesterol levels. Good sources of monounsaturated fat are olive oil, avocados and peanuts. The polyunsaturated fats are found in large quantities in sunflower oil, soya oil and corn oil. So, the basic guidelines are: eat less red meat and eat only lean meat, always skin chicken, avoid too many eggs, and use low-fat milk, low-fat cheeses such as cottage cheese, and olive, sunflower, and peanut oils and margarines.

What you do eat is as important as what you avoid. There are some foods that are actually thought to bring down blood cholesterol levels and these should be eaten freely in the diet. These include oat bran, dried peas and beans, barley, brown rice, and oily fish such as salmon, mackerel, anchovies and sardines. Eating less cholesterol-inducing foods need in no way be a chore. It is simply a matter of re-educating your palate, and becoming more aware of fats in your diet. The recipes here demonstrate how delicious low-cholesterol cooking can be, with plenty of soups, salads, oily fish, chicken, turkey and, as in every healthy diet, plenty of fresh fruit and vegetables.

CELERY AND APPLE SOUP

This interesting combination of flavours produces a tasty soup which contains no saturated fat whatsoever.

SERVES 4

30g/1oz polyunsaturated margarine
1 large onion, finely chopped
3 cooking apples, peeled, cored and sliced
1.2 litres/2 pints vegetable stock
1 bay leaf
Salt and freshly ground black pepper
3 sticks of celery, finely chopped
Finely sliced celery, for garnish

1. Melt the margarine in a large pan and stir in the onion. Sauté gently for 5 minutes, or until the onion is soft but not browned.

2. Add the apples to the pan and cook for a further 3 minutes, or until the apples begin to soften.

3. Stir half the stock into the onion and apples along with the bay leaf and seasoning. Bring the mixture to the boil, cover and simmer for 30 minutes. Remove the bay leaf.

4. Put the remaining stock into another pan along with the celery. Bring to the boil, then cover and simmer for 30 minutes.

5. Using a liquidiser or food processor, blend the onion and apple mixture until it is smooth.

6. Whisk the puréed mixture into the pan containing the stock and celery.

7. Return the pan to the heat and bring back to the boil. Garnish with the celery and serve immediately.

TIME: Preparation takes about 15 minutes, cooking takes about 45 minutes.

SERVING IDEAS: Serve with wholemeal rolls or a French stick.

TO FREEZE: This soup freezes well. Measure into large freezer-proof containers or freezer-bags allowing plenty of room for expansion.

VICHYSSOISE

Although this French soup is usually eaten cold, it is also delicious served hot.

SERVES 4

3 large leeks
30g/1oz polyunsaturated margarine
1 medium onion, sliced
2 medium potatoes, peeled and thinly
   sliced
570ml/1 pint vegetable stock
Salt and ground white pepper
280ml/½ pint skimmed milk
Finely chopped parsley or chives, for
   garnish

1. Trim the top and bottom from the leeks and peel away the outer leaf.

2. Slit the leeks lengthways down one side cutting right into the centre of the vegetable.

3. Rinse under cold running water, to wash out any soil or grit from in between the leaves. Drain, then slice the leeks very thinly using a sharp knife.

4. Melt the margarine in a saucepan and add the leeks and sliced onion. Cover and allow to sweat gently over a low heat for about 10 minutes.

5. Add the potatoes to the leek mixture and pour in the stock. Season with the salt and pepper, cover and cook gently for 15 minutes, or until the potatoes are tender.

6. Using a liquidiser or food processor, purée the soup until it is smooth.

7. Return the puréed soup to the saucepan and stir in the milk. Adjust the seasoning and reheat very gently until it is almost boiling. Remove from the heat.

8. Either serve the soup immediately or allow to cool, then chill in a refrigerator for at least 2 hours. Serve garnished with the finely chopped parsley or chives.

TIME: Preparation takes about 15 minutes, plus chilling time. Cooking takes about 30 minutes.

SERVING IDEA: Serve with lightly toasted slices of wholemeal bread.

SMOKED MACKEREL PÂTÉ

Smoked fish has a wonderful flavour and is ideal for making pâté. Fish also contains monounsaturated fat which does not affect the cholesterol level of the blood.

SERVES 4

225g/8oz smoked mackerel fillets, skin and bones removed
60g/2oz polyunsaturated margarine
Juice of ½ orange
1 tsp tomato purée
1 tsp white wine vinegar
Salt and freshly ground black pepper, optional
1 × 113g/3½oz can pimento peppers, drained
280ml/½ pint clear vegetable stock
2 tsps powdered gelatine
2 tbsps dry sherry
2 tbsps cold water

1. Put the mackerel, margarine, orange juice, tomato purée, vinegar and seasoning into a liquidiser or food processor and blend until smooth.

2. Put the pâté into a serving dish and smooth the top evenly.

3. Cut the pimento into thin strips and arrange in a lattice over the top of the pâté.

4. Bring the stock to the boil in a small pan. Remove from the heat and cool for 1 minute.

5. Sprinkle over the gelatine and allow to stand, stirring occasionally until it has completely dissolved.

6. When the gelatine has dissolved the liquid should be clear. At this point stir in the sherry and cold water.

7. Very carefully spoon the aspic over the top of the mackerel pâté and the pimentos, taking great care not to dislodge the lattice pattern.

8. Chill the pâté in a refrigerator until the aspic has completely set.

TIME: Preparation takes about 30 minutes, plus chilling time. Cooking takes about 2 minutes.

VARIATION: Use any type of smoked fish in place of the mackerel in this recipe.

PREPARATION: If you do not have a food processor or blender, this pâté can be made by mashing with a fork, but it will not have such a smooth texture.

SERVING IDEAS: Serve with crusty wholemeal bread or French toast.

SPICY VEGETABLE FRITTERS

This delicious dish makes an ideal starter or interesting snack.

SERVES 4-6

120g/4oz plain flour
120g/4oz wholemeal flour
1 tsp salt
1 tsp chilli powder
1 tsp ground cumin
280ml/½ pint water
1 tbsp lemon juice
1 small cauliflower, broken into small florets
1 aubergine, cut into 2.5cm/1-inch cubes
3 courgettes, trimmed and cut into 2.5cm/
    1-inch pieces
225g/8oz button mushrooms
1 red and 1 green pepper, cut into 5mm/
    ¼-inch thick rings
1 large potato, peeled and cut into 2.5cm/
    1-inch cubes
1 × 400g/14oz can plum tomatoes, drained
1 red chilli, seeded and chopped
1 clove garlic, crushed
1 small onion, finely chopped
1 tbsp white wine vinegar
1 tbsp soft brown sugar
Salt the freshly ground black pepper
Sliced chillies, for garnish
Vegetable oil, for deep frying

1. Sift the flours, salt, chilli powder and cumin into a bowl. Make a well in the centre. Gradually add the water and lemon juice, beating well until a smooth batter is formed.

2. Wash the prepared vegetables and drain completely on kitchen paper.

3. Blend the tomatoes, chilli, garlic, onion, vinegar and sugar in a food processor or liquidiser until smooth.

4. Pour into a small pan and heat gently, stirring until warmed through. Season then transfer to a small serving dish and garnish with sliced chillies.

5. Heat some vegetable oil in a deep-fat fryer until it will brown a 2.5cm/1-inch cube of bread in just under 1 minute.

6. Make sure the vegetables are completely dry – pat off any moisture if necessary.

7. Using a slotted spoon drop a few vegetables into the batter and coat thoroughly. Remove from the batter, with the spoon, to allow some batter to drain back.

8. Drop the vegetables into the oil, and fry quickly until golden brown and puffy.

9. Remove the fritters from the oil and drain on kitchen paper, keeping them warm until all the remaining fritters are made. Serve immediately with the spicy tomato sauce.

TIME: Preparation takes about 20 minutes, cooking takes about ½ hour.

WATCHPOINT: It is important to ensure that the vegetables are completely dry before coating with the batter, or it will not cover them.

COOK'S TIP: Check that the oil used for the deep-fat frying is polyunsaturated.

TOMATO AND PEPPER ICE

Similar to frozen gazpacho, this starter is ideal for serving on warm summer days. It could also be used, in smaller quantities, as a palate freshener between courses.

SERVES 4-6

6 ice cubes
120ml/4 fl oz canned tomato juice
Juice 1 lemon
1 tsp Worcestershire sauce
½ small green pepper, roughly chopped
½ small red pepper, roughly chopped

1. Put the ice into a thick plastic bag or a tea-towel and break into small pieces using a small hammer.

2. Put the broken ice into a blender or food processor along with the tomato juice, lemon juice and Worcestershire sauce. Blend the mixture until it becomes slushy.

3. Pour the tomato mixture into ice trays or other shallow containers and freeze for ½ hour, or until it is just half frozen.

4. Using a sharp knife, chop the peppers into very small pieces.

5. Remove the tomato ice from the trays and put it into a bowl.

6. Mash the tomato ice with the back of a fork until the crystals are well broken up.

7. Mix in the chopped peppers and return the tomato ice to the trays.

8. Re-freeze for a further 1½ hours, stirring occasionally to prevent the mixture from solidifying completely.

9. To serve, allow the tomato ice to defrost for about 5 minutes, then mash with the back of a fork to roughly break up the ice crystals. Serve in small glass dishes which have been chilled beforehand.

TIME: Preparation takes about 15 minutes, plus freezing time.

WATCHPOINT: Take care not to allow the tomato ice to freeze into a solid block or it will be too hard to break into rough crystals.

SERVING IDEAS: Cut the tops off some tomatoes, scoop the middle and serve this ice in the tomato shells.

SUMMER PASTA SALAD

Lightly cooked summer vegetables and wholemeal pasta are combined to create this delicious, wholesome salad.

SERVES 4

1 aubergine
1 courgette
1 red pepper
1 green pepper
1 medium onion
2 large tomatoes
60ml/4 tbsps olive oil
1 clove garlic, crushed
Salt and freshly ground black pepper
225g/8oz wholemeal pasta spirals
1 tbsp vinegar
½ tsp English mustard powder

1. Cut the aubergine into 1.25cm/½-inch slices. Sprinkle the slices liberally with salt and allow to stand for 30 minutes.

2. Using a sharp knife, trim the courgette and cut into 5mm/¼-inch slices.

3. Cut the peppers in half and carefully remove the cores and seeds. Using a sharp knife, cut the pepper into thin strips.

4. Peel and finely chop the onion.

5. Cut a small cross in the skins of the tomatoes and plunge them into boiling water for 30 seconds. Drain, then carefully peel off the skins.

6. Cut the tomatoes into 8, discarding the pips.

7. Put 2 tbsps of the olive oil in a frying pan and stir in the onion. Sauté gently until transparent, but not coloured.

8. Thoroughly rinse the salt from the aubergine slices and pat dry on kitchen paper. Roughly chop the slices.

9. Add the chopped aubergine, courgette, peppers, tomatoes and garlic to the cooked onion and cook very gently for 20 minutes, or until just soft. Season with salt and pepper and allow to cool.

10. Put the pasta spirals in a large saucepan and cover with boiling water. Sprinkle in a little salt. Bring to the boil, stir and simmer for 10 minutes or until 'al dente'.

11. Rinse the pasta in cold water and drain very well.

12. Whisk together the remaining olive oil, the vinegar and mustard in a small bowl. Season with salt and pepper.

13. Put the pasta and cooled vegetables into a serving dish and pour over the dressing, tossing the ingredients together to coat them evenly. Serve well chilled.

TIME: Preparation takes approximately 40 minutes, cooking takes 30 minutes.

PREPARATION: Make sure that the aubergine is rinsed very thoroughly or the salad will be much too salty.

CHINESE SALAD

Salad is not a part of Chinese cuisine, but certain Chinese vegetables mixed together and tossed in a soy sauce dressing make an interesting, crunchy salad.

SERVES 4-6

Bunch of radishes
225g/8oz Chinese leaves
120g/4oz bean sprouts
120g/4oz canned bamboo shoots, thinly sliced
120g/4oz canned water chestnuts, thinly sliced
1 stick celery, thinly sliced
60g/2oz mushrooms, wiped and thinly sliced
1 tbsp chopped chives or spring onions, for garnish

Dressing
90g/3oz spring onions (green part only), finely chopped
140ml/¼ pint rice vinegar or white wine vinegar

2 tbsps soy sauce
200ml/7 fl oz groundnut oil
2 tbsps sesame oil
2 tsps sugar
1 tsp salt
½ tsp ground ginger

1. One hour before preparing the salad, finely slice the radishes almost through with a knife and put in the refrigerator in a bowl of cold water.

2. Shred the Chinese leaves and put them into a salad bowl together with the other vegetables. Drain the radishes and add.

3. Put all the dressing ingredients into a screw-top jar and shake well until blended. Just before serving, pour the dressing over the salad and toss well. Scatter the chives over and serve.

TIME: Preparation takes 20 minutes, plus 1 hour soaking time.

SERVING IDEA: Serve with a stir-fry dish.

BUTTER BEAN, LEMON AND FENNEL SALAD

This interesting combination of textures and flavours makes an unusual lunch or supper dish.

SERVES 4

225g/8oz butter beans, soaked overnight
1 lemon
1 large bulb fennel, thinly sliced
60ml/4 tbsps vegetable or soya oil
Pinch sugar
Salt and freshly ground black pepper
Lettuce and radicchio leaves, to serve

1. Place the butter beans and enough water to cover them by 2.5cm/1-inch, into a saucepan and bring to the boil. Boil rapidly for 10 minutes, then reduce the heat and simmer gently for about 2 hours or until the beans are tender; drain well.

2. Pare the rind from the lemon in strips, taking care not to include too much white pith. Cut the rind into very thin shreds.

3. Blanch the lemon shreds for 5 minutes in boiling water. Remove from the water with a draining spoon.

4. Add the fennel to the water (reserve the green tops) and blanch for 2 minutes – the fennel should be just cooked but still crunchy to the bite.

5. Squeeze the juice from the lemon and place in a bowl with lemon shreds, oil, sugar and seasoning. Whisk together with a fork. Chop the reserved fennel tops and add to the dressing.

6. Mix the cooked beans and fennel in a large bowl, then add the dressing and toss to coat the vegetables. Serve on a bed of lettuce and radicchio leaves.

TIME: Preparation takes about 10 minutes, plus overnight soaking. Cooking time is about 2 hours.

SERVING IDEAS: Serve with boiled new potatoes or jacket potatoes.

PENNE WITH SPICY CHILLI SAUCE

*Penne are hollow pasta tubes which can be bought at most supermarkets.
Macaroni can be used equally as well.*

SERVES 4-6

460g/1lb canned plum tomatoes
1 tbsp olive oil
2 cloves garlic, crushed
1 onion, chopped
2 red chillies, seeded and chopped
2 spring onions, chopped
60g/2oz pecorino or Parmesan cheese,
    grated
460g/1lb penne or macaroni
Salt and pepper

1. Chop the tomatoes and sieve them to remove the pips.

2. Heat the oil in a frying pan and gently sauté the garlic and onion for 6-8 minutes.

3. Add the sieved tomatoes, the chillies, chopped spring onions and half of the cheese. Simmer gently for 20 minutes. Season to taste.

4. Cook the penne or macaroni in boiling water for 10-15 minutes, or until 'al dente'. Rinse under hot water and drain well.

5. Put the cooked penne into a warm serving dish and toss them in half of the sauce. Pour the remaining sauce over the top and sprinkle with the remaining cheese.

TIME: Preparation takes about 15 minutes and cooking takes about 30 minutes.

SERVING IDEAS: Garnish the serving dish with spring onions and serve with a mixed green salad.

NOODLES WITH GINGER AND OYSTER SAUCE

Noodles stir-fried with ginger, carrot and courgette, then served in an oyster sauce make a delicious accompaniment to chicken.

SERVES 4

225g/8oz Chinese noodles
1 carrot
1 courgette
1 piece fresh root ginger
1 tbsp oil
1 spring onion, cut into thin rounds
1 tbsp soy sauce
2 tbsps oyster sauce
Salt and pepper

1. Cook the noodles in boiling, salted water for 10 minutes until tender, then rinse them under cold water and set aside to drain.

2. Cut the carrot into thin strips. Thickly peel the courgette to include some of the flesh and cut into thin strips. Discard the centre of the courgette.

3. Peel the ginger sparingly, but remove any hard parts. Pare off 3 thin slices using a potato peeler. Cut the slices into thin shreds using a very sharp knife.

4. Heat the oil in a wok and stir-fry the spring onion for 10 seconds. Add the carrot, courgette and ginger and stir-fry briefly.

5. Stir in the noodles and cook for 1 minute. Stir in the soy and oyster sauces, and continue cooking until heated through. Season with salt and pepper and serve.

TIME: Preparation takes about 15 minutes and cooking takes about 15 minutes.

VARIATION: Cook the noodles in chicken stock instead of salted water to give them extra flavour.

WATCHPOINT: Stir-fry the ginger and the other vegetables very quickly to avoid browning them. Lower the heat if necessary.

CHICKPEA SALAD

This simple starter combines squid and chick peas in garlic and shallot sauce.

SERVES 4

300g/11oz dried chickpeas
1 carrot, cut into 4
1 onion stuck with 2 cloves
Sprig thyme
1 bay leaf
1 prepared squid
1 tbsp chopped parsley
1 clove garlic, chopped
1 shallot, chopped
1 tbsp wine vinegar
3 tbsps olive oil
Salt and pepper

1. Soak the chickpeas overnight in plenty of cold water.

2. Drain the peas and put them in a saucepan with salted boiling water, the carrot, onion, thyme and the bay leaf.

3. Bring to the boil, then reduce the heat and simmer for about 2 hours, depending on how you prefer your chickpeas.

4. Cook the prepared squid in a steamer for about 4 minutes, or until tender. Cut the cooked squid into thin rings.

5. Make a sauce by mixing together the parsley, garlic, shallot, vinegar and the olive oil. Season to taste.

6. When the peas are cooked through, remove the onion, carrot, bay leaf and thyme and discard. Rinse the peas in cold water and set aside to drain.

7. Once the peas are cold, combine them with the squid and the sauce. Serve at room temperature on individual plates.

TIME: Preparation takes about 10 minutes, plus overnight soaking for the peas, and total cooking time is about 2 hours and 10 minutes.

WATCHPOINT: It is essential to soak the chickpeas overnight, otherwise cooking will take much longer.

VEGETABLE STEW WITH HERB DUMPLINGS

The ideal meal to warm up a cold winter's night.

SERVES 4-6

1 large onion
900g/2lbs mixed vegetables (carrot, swede,
    parsnips, turnips, cauliflower etc.)
570ml/1 pint stock or water plus a stock
    cube
Salt and pepper
Cornflour, to thicken

Dumplings
120g/4oz wholewheat self-raising flour
60g/2oz vegetarian suet
1 tsp mixed herbs
¼ tsp salt

1. Chop the onion into large pieces.
2. Peel and prepare the vegetables and chop into bite-sized pieces.

3. Put the onion and vegetables into a pan and cover with the stock.
4. Bring to the boil and simmer for 20 minutes.
5. Season to taste.
6. Mix a little cornflour with a little water and stir into the stew to thicken.
7. Place the ingredients for the dumplings into a bowl and add just enough water to bind to a stiff dough.
8. Shape the mixture into 8 small dumplings.
9. Bring the stew to the boil and drop in the dumplings.
10. Cover and allow to simmer for 20 minutes. Serve at once.

TIME: Preparation takes 10 minutes, cooking takes about 40 minutes.

SERVING IDEA: Serve with boiled or mashed potatoes.

VARIATION: The mixed herbs may be omitted when making the dumplings or chopped fresh parsley and a squeeze of lemon juice may be used instead.

MIXED PEPPER SALAD

Although this recipe is high in polyunsaturated fat, the eggs do contain some saturated fat in the yolks, but they may be omitted if wished.

SERVES 6-8

3 red peppers
3 green peppers
3 yellow peppers
2 tbsps vegetable oil
90ml/6 tbsps sunflower oil
2 tbsps lemon juice
2 tbsps white wine vinegar
1 small clove garlic, crushed
Pinch salt
Pinch cayenne pepper
Pinch sugar
3 hard-boiled eggs (optional)
60g/2oz black olives, pitted
2 tbsps finely chopped fresh coriander
    leaves (optional)

1. Cut all the peppers in half and remove the seeds and cores.

2. With the palm of your hand lightly press the halved peppers down onto a flat surface to flatten them out.

3. Brush the skin side of each pepper with a little of the vegetable oil and place under a preheated hot grill.

4. Cook until the skins begin to char and split.

5. Remove the peppers from the grill and wrap them in a clean tea-towel. Allow to stand for 10-15 minutes.

6. Put the sunflower oil, lemon juice, vinegar, garlic, salt, cayenne pepper and sugar into a small bowl and whisk together well.

7. Shell the eggs and cut each one into four, lengthwise.

8. Unwrap the peppers and carefully peel away the burnt skin. Cut the pepper flesh into thick strips about 2.5cm/1-inch wide.

9. Arrange the pepper strips in a circle on a serving plate, alternating the colours all the way round.

10. Arrange the olives and quartered eggs in the centre.

11. Sprinkle with the coriander leaves and spoon over all the dressing.

12. Chill the salad for at least 1 hour before serving.

TIME: Preparation takes 20 minutes, cooking takes about 5 minutes.

SERVING IDEAS: Serve this salad with crusty French bread or rolls.

COOK'S TIP: Skinned peppers will keep in a refrigerator for up to 5 days if they are covered with a little oil.

LENTIL AND VEGETABLE CURRY

Lentils are a staple ingredient in Indian cookery. This delicious vegetable curry should be made using fresh spices for the best flavour.

SERVES 4

225g/8oz whole green lentils
2 tbsps vegetable oil
½ tsp mustard seeds, crushed
1 tsp ground coriander
½ tsp ground cumin
2 dried red chillies, crushed
1 carrot, peeled and sliced diagonally
1 potato, peeled and cubed
6-8 okra, topped and tailed, then cut into
    2.5cm/1-inch pieces
1 small courgette, sliced diagonally
1 small aubergine, halved and sliced
420ml/¾ pint water
1 tsp salt
6 curry leaves
1 green chilli, slit in half and chopped
1 tsp fresh chopped mint
1 tbsp fresh chopped coriander
Coriander leaves, to garnish

1. Wash the lentils in warm water until it runs clear. Drain well. Put into a large saucepan and pour over 570ml/1 pint water. Simmer gently for 15-20 minutes.

2. When the lentils are soft, beat with a potato masher or whisk until they are puréed.

3. In a large saucepan heat the oil and gently fry the mustard seeds, ground coriander, cumin and dried chillies for 1 minute.

4. Add the vegetables to the spices and cook for 2 minutes, stirring all the time, to coat them evenly in the oil and spice mixture.

5. Add the water, salt and the puréed lentils to the vegetable mixture and stir well.

6. Add the curry leaves, chopped chilli, mint and fresh coriander, then cook for 15 minutes. Serve hot, garnished with coriander leaves.

TIME: Preparation takes about 10 minutes, cooking takes 20-30 minutes.

VARIATION: Use any combination of fresh vegetables to vary this curry.

SERVING IDEA: Serve with boiled basmati rice.

ORANGE, GRAPEFRUIT AND MINT SALAD

Fresh citrus fruits are complemented beautifully by the fragrant flavour of fresh mint.

SERVES 4

2 grapefruits
3 oranges
Sugar to taste (optional)
8 sprigs of mint

1. Using a serrated knife, cut away the peel and all the white pith from the grapefruit and the oranges.

2. Carefully cut either side of the membranes surrounding the sections of flesh to remove each segment of flesh.

3. Squeeze the membranes over a bowl to extract all the juice. Sweeten the juice with a little sugar if required.

4. Arrange the orange and the grapefruit segments in alternating colours on 4 individual serving dishes.

5. Using a sharp knife, chop 4 sprigs of the mint very finely. Stir the chopped mint into the fruit juice.

6. Carefully spoon the juice over the arranged fruit segments and chill thoroughly.

7. Garnish with a sprig of mint before serving.

TIME: Preparation takes about 20 minutes, plus chilling time.

COOK'S TIP: This starter can be prepared up to a day in advance.

PREPARATION: Make sure all the white pith is removed from the fruit, as it produces a bitter flavour.

VARIATION: Use ruby grapefruits and blood oranges, when available, in place of the normal types of fruit for a colourful variation. Use borage leaves in place of the mint and garnish with a few of the blue flowers.

MUSHROOM PASTA SALAD

Mushrooms are always delicious in a salad and this recipe, which combines them with wholemeal pasta shapes, is no exception.

SERVES 4

75ml/5 tbsps olive oil
Juice of 2 lemons
1 tsp fresh chopped basil
1 tsp fresh chopped parsley
Salt and freshly ground black pepper
225g/8oz mushrooms
225g/8oz wholemeal pasta shapes of your
    choice

1. In a large bowl mix together the olive oil, lemon juice, herbs and seasoning.

2. Finely slice the mushrooms and add these to the lemon dressing in the bowl, stirring well to coat the mushrooms evenly.

3. Cover the bowl with cling film and allow to stand in a cool place for at least 1 hour.

4. Put the pasta into a large saucepan and cover with boiling water. Season with a little salt and simmer for 10-12 minutes, or until 'al dente'.

5. Rinse the pasta in cold water and drain well.

6. Add the pasta to the marinated mushrooms and lemon dressing, mixing well to coat evenly.

7. Adjust the seasoning if necessary, then chill well before serving.

TIME: Preparation takes about 10 minutes, plus at least 1 hour for the mushrooms to marinate. Cooking takes about 15 minutes.

VARIATION: Use a mixture of button and wild mushrooms for a delicious variation in flavour.

SERVING IDEAS: Serve mushroom pasta salad on a bed of mixed lettuce.

STIR-FRY TOFU SALAD

Ideal for vegetarians, but so delicious that it will be enjoyed by everyone.

SERVES 4-6

1 packet tofu
120g/4oz mange tout peas
60g/2oz mushrooms
2 carrots, peeled
2 sticks celery
4 spring onions
60g/2oz broccoli florets
90ml/6 tbsps vegetable oil
1½ tbsps lemon juice
1 tsp honey
½ tsp grated fresh ginger
1½ tbsps soy sauce
Dash of sesame oil
60g/2oz unsalted roasted peanuts
120g/4oz bean sprouts
½ head Chinese leaves

1. Drain the tofu well and press gently to remove any excess moisture. Cut into 1.25cm/½-inch cubes.

2. Trim the tops and tails from the mange tout peas.

3. Thinly slice the mushrooms with a sharp knife.

4. Cut the carrots and celery into thin slices, angling your knife so that each slice is cut on the diagonal.

5. Trim the spring onions and slice them in the same way as the carrots and celery. Break the broccoli into small florets.

6. Heat 2 tbsps of the vegetable oil in a wok or large frying pan. Stir in the mange tout, mushrooms, celery, carrots and broccoli and cook for 2 minutes, stirring constantly.

7. Remove the vegetables from the wok and set them aside to cool.

8. Put the remaining oil into a small bowl and whisk in the lemon juice, honey, ginger, soy sauce and sesame oil.

9. Stir the sliced spring onions, peanuts and bean sprouts into the cooled vegetables.

10. Mix the dressing into the salad vegetables, then add the tofu. Toss the tofu into the salad very carefully so that it does not break up.

11. Shred the Chinese leaves and arrange them on a serving platter. Pile the salad ingredients over the top and serve well chilled.

TIME: Preparation takes about 25 minutes, cooking takes 2-4 minutes.

PREPARATION: Make sure that the stir-fried vegetables are completely cool before adding the remaining salad ingredients, or they will lose their crispness.

VARIATION: Shredded cooked chicken can be used in place of the tofu in this recipe for non vegetarians.

BLACK-EYED BEAN AND ORANGE SALAD

This colourful salad has a fresh taste which is given a delicious peppery 'bite' by the addition of watercress.

SERVES 4-6

225g/8oz black-eyed beans, soaked
   overnight
1 bay leaf
1 slice onion
Juice and grated rind of 1 orange
75ml/5 tbsps olive oil
6 black olives, pitted and quartered
4 spring onions, trimmed and chopped
2 tbsps chopped fresh parsley
2 tbsps chopped fresh basil
Salt and freshly ground black pepper
4 whole oranges
1 bunch watercress, washed

1. Place the beans, bay leaf, onion slice and enough water to cover by 2.5cm/1-inch in a saucepan and bring to the boil. Boil rapidly for 10 minutes, then reduce the heat and simmer gently for about 50 minutes-1 hour, or until the beans are tender. Drain well.

2. Put the orange juice, rind and oil in a small bowl and whisk together with a fork. Stir in the olives, spring onions and chopped herbs into the dressing.

3. Add the cooked beans to the dressing and season with salt and pepper. Mix thoroughly to coat the beans well.

4. Cut off the rind and all the pith of the oranges, then segment the flesh. Chop the segments of 3 of the oranges and add to the beans.

5. Arrange the watercress on individual serving plates and pile equal amounts of the bean and orange salad on top.

6. Arrange the remaining orange slices on the plate as a garnish and serve immediately.

TIME: Preparation takes about 20 minutes, plus overnight soaking. Cooking time is about 1 hour.

SERVING IDEAS: Serve with wholemeal pitta bread or taco shells.

43

SPAGHETTI MARINARA

This delightful recipe is perfect for special occasions or as a weekend treat.

SERVES 4

45g/1½oz can anchovy fillets
75ml/5 tbsps water
75ml/5 tbsps dry white wine
1 bay leaf
4 peppercorns
460g/1lb scallops, cleaned and sliced
2 tbsps olive oil
2 cloves garlic, crushed
1 tsp basil
1 × 400g/14oz can plum tomatoes, seeded and chopped
1 tbsp tomato purée
275g/10oz spaghetti
225g/8oz cooked prawns, shelled and de-veined
2 tbsps chopped parsley
Salt and pepper

1. Drain anchovies well and cut them into small pieces. Set aside.

2. Place the water, wine, bay leaf and peppercorns in a pan. Heat to a slow boil. Add the scallops and cook for 2 minutes. Remove and drain.

3. Heat the oil, add the garlic and basil and cook for 30 seconds.

4. Add tomatoes, anchovies and tomato purée to the garlic. Stir until combined. Cook for 10 minutes.

5. Meanwhile, cook the spaghetti in a large pan of boiling, salted water for 10 minutes, or until 'al dente'. Drain well.

6. Add the prawns and scallops to the sauce and cook a further minute. Add half the parsley and stir through. Season with salt and pepper to taste. Toss gently.

7. Pour the sauce over the spaghetti and serve immediately, sprinkled with remaining parsley.

TIME: Preparation takes 10 minutes, cooking takes 20 minutes.

SINGAPORE FISH

The cuisine of Singapore was much influenced by that of China. In turn, the Chinese brought ingredients like curry powder into their own cuisine.

SERVES 6

450g/1lb whitefish fillets

1 egg white

1 tbsp cornflour

2 tsps white wine

Salt and pepper

Oil for frying

1 large onion, cut into 1.25cm/½ inch-thick wedges

1 tbsp mild curry powder

1 small can pineapple pieces, drained and juice reserved, or ½ fresh pineapple, peeled and cubed

1 small can mandarin orange segments, drained and juice reserved

1 small can sliced water chestnuts, drained

1 tbsp cornflour mixed with juice of 1 lime

2 tsps sugar (optional)

1. Starting at the tail end of the fillets, skin them using a sharp knife.

2. Slide the knife back and forth along the length of each fillet, pushing the fish flesh along as you go.

3. Cut the fish into even-sized pieces, about 5cm/2 inches.

4. Mix together the egg white, cornflour, wine, salt and pepper. Place the fish in the mixture and leave to stand while heating the oil.

5. When the oil is hot, fry a few pieces of fish at a time until light golden brown and crisp. Remove the fish to paper towels to drain, and continue until all the fish is cooked.

6. Remove all but 1 tbsp of the oil from the wok and add the onion. Stir-fry the onion for 1-2 minutes and add the curry powder. Cook the onion and curry powder for a further 1-2 minutes. Add the juice from the pineapple and mandarin oranges and bring to the boil.

7. Combine the cornflour and lime juice and add a spoonful of the boiling fruit juice. Return the mixture to the wok and cook until thickened, about 2 minutes. Taste and add sugar if desired. Add the fruit, water chestnuts and fried fish to the wok and stir to coat. Heat through 1 minute and serve immediately.

TIME Preparation takes about 25 minutes, cooking takes about 10 minutes.

COD CURRY

The fragrant spices used in this recipe are now readily available at most supermarkets.

SERVES 4

---

3 tbsps vegetable oil

1 large onion, chopped

2.5cm/1-inch piece cinnamon stick

1 bay leaf

1 tsp ginger paste

1 tsp garlic paste

1 tsp chilli powder

1 tsp ground cumin

1 tsp ground coriander

¼ tsp ground turmeric

140ml/¼ pint natural low fat yogurt OR
    225g/8oz canned tomatoes, chopped

1-2 fresh green chillies, chopped

2 sprigs fresh coriander leaves, chopped

460g/1lb cod cutlets or fillets, cut into
    5cm/2-inch pieces

1 tsp salt

1. Heat the oil in a large heavy-based saucepan, add the onion and sauté until golden brown. Add the cinnamon, bay leaf and the ginger and garlic pastes and cook for 1 minute.

2. Add the ground spices and fry for a further minute, the stir in *either* the yogurt, *or* the canned tomatoes and the chopped chillies and coriander leaves.

3. Only if you have used yogurt, stir in 140ml/¼ pint water and simmer the mixture for 2-3 minutes. Do not add any water if you have used the tomatoes.

4. Stir the cod into the sauce and add the salt. Cover the pan and simmer for 15-18 minutes before serving.

TIME: Preparation takes about 15 minutes, and cooking takes about 20 minutes.

COOK'S TIP: Great care should be taken when preparing fresh chillies. Always wash hands thoroughly afterwards, and avoid getting any neat juice in the eyes or mouth. Rinse with copious amounts of clear water, if this happens. For a milder curry, remove the seeds; for a hotter curry, leave them in.

SERVING IDEAS: Serve with boiled rice and a cucumber salad.

GRILLED FISH

Grilling fish with herbs and lemon is one of the most delightful ways of preparing it, and is a particularly popular method in the Mediterranean.

SERVES 4

2 large bream or other whole fish, cleaned
Salt and pepper
Lemon juice
Sprigs of fresh thyme and oregano
Olive oil
Lemon wedges
Vine leaves, fresh or preserved in brine
   (optional)

1. Rinse the fish, pat dry and sprinkle the cavity with salt, pepper and lemon juice. Place sprigs of herbs inside.

2. Make 3 diagonal cuts on the side of the fish with a sharp knife. Place the fish on a grill rack and sprinkle with olive oil and more lemon juice.

3. Cook under a preheated grill for about 8-10 minutes per side, until golden brown and crisp. The exact cooking time will depend on the thickness of the fish.

4. If using vine leaves preserved in brine, rinse them well. If using fresh vine leaves, pour over boiling water and leave to stand for about 10 minutes to soften slightly. Drain and allow to cool. Line a large serving platter with the vine leaves and when the fish is cooked, place it on top of the leaves. Serve surrounded with lemon wedges.

TIME: Preparation takes about 20 minutes, cooking takes about 16-20 minutes, depending upon the size of the fish.

COOK'S TIP: When grilling large whole fish, slit the skin on both sides to help the fish cook evenly.

VARIATION: The fish may be wrapped in vine leaves before grilling. This keeps the fish moist and adds extra flavour. Other fish suitable for cooking by this method are red mullet, trout, sea bass, grey mullet, sardines, herring or mackerel.

PREPARATION: If wished, the fish may be cooked on an outdoor barbecue grill. Wait until the coals have white ash on the top and be sure to oil the rack before placing on the fish, or use a special wire cage for cooking fish.

PAELLA

This dish has as many variations as Spain has cooks! Fish, meat and poultry combine with vegetables and rice to make a complete meal.

SERVES 6

12 mussels in their shells

6 clams (if not available use 6 more mussels)

6 king prawns

2 chorizos or other spicy sausages

3 tbsps olive oil

900g/2lb chicken cut in 12 serving-size pieces

1 small onion, chopped

1 clove garlic, crushed

2 small peppers, red and green, diced

460g/1lb long grain rice

Large pinch of saffron

1.15 litres/2 pints boiling water

Salt and pepper

175g/6oz cod, skinned and cut into 5cm/ 2-inch pieces

150g/5oz frozen peas

3 tomatoes, skinned, seeded and chopped

1. Scrub the mussels and clams well to remove beards and barnacles. Discard any with broken shells or those that do not close when tapped. Leave the mussels and clams to soak in water with a handful of flour for 30 minutes.

2. Remove the heads and legs from the prawns, if wished, but leave on the tail shells.

3. Place the sausage in a saucepan and cover with water. Bring to the boil and then simmer for 5 minutes. Drain and slice into 5mm/¼-inch rounds. Set aside.

4. Heat the oil and sauté the chicken pieces, browning evenly on both sides. Remove and drain on kitchen paper.

5. Add the sausage, onion, garlic and peppers to the pan and cook briskly for about 3 minutes.

6. Combine the sausage mixture with the rice and saffron and place in a special Paella dish or a large oven and flame-proof casserole. Pour on the water, season with salt and pepper and bring to the boil. Stir occasionally and allow to boil for about 2 minutes.

7. Add the chicken pieces and place in an oven preheated to 200°C/400°F/Gas Mark 6, for about 15 minutes.

8. Add the clams, mussels, prawns, cod and peas and cook a further 10-15 minutes or until the rice is tender, chicken is cooked and mussels and clams open. Discard any that do not open. Add the tomatoes 5 minutes before the end of cooking time and serve immediately.

TIME: Preparation takes about 30-40 minutes, cooking takes about 35-40 minutes.

TROUT IN ASPIC

This attractive main course is ideal for serving as a part of a summer's meal.

SERVES 4

1.7 litres/3 pints water
Pinch salt
6 black peppercorns
2 bay leaves
2 sprigs fresh parsley
1 small onion, quartered
280ml/½ pint dry white wine
4 rainbow trout, gutted and well washed
2 egg whites, softly beaten
2 tbsps powdered gelatine
Lemon slices, capers and dill, to garnish

---

1. Put the water, salt, peppercorns, bay leaves, parsley, onion and wine into a large saucepan or fish kettle. Bring to the boil and simmer for about 30 minutes.

2. Cool slightly, then lay the fish in the hot stock. Cover the pan and bring back to simmering point.

3. Cook the fish gently for 5 minutes, then remove from the heat. Allow the fish to cool in the covered pan then drain on kitchen paper. Reserve the stock.

4. Using a sharp knife, carefully peel away the skin from the cooked fish.

5. Using a palette knife, lift the fillets from the top of each fish, taking great care that they do not break, and lay them on a large serving plate that has a raised lip.

6. Lift the backbone away from the lower fillets and discard. Arrange the lower fish fillets on the serving plate along with the others.

7. Strain the reserved fish stock into a large saucepan through a fine nylon sieve to remove the spices, herbs and vegetables.

8. Add the egg whites to the fish stock and heat gently, whisking constantly with a balloon whisk. The egg whites should form a thick frothy crust on top.

9. Bring the mixture to the boil then stop whisking and allow the mixture to rise up the sides of the pan. Remove from the heat and allow to subside. Repeat this process twice more, then allow to settle completely.

10. Line a colander with several layers of kitchen paper or muslin and stand it over a large bowl. Pour the fish stock into the colander along with the egg whites and allow to drain slowly. Do not allow the egg whites to fall into the clarified liquid.

11. When the liquid has drained through, remove about 140ml/¼ pint and heat it gently. Sprinkle the gelatine over and allow to stand until it has dissolved completely.

12. Mix the gelatine mixture into the remaining stock, to make aspic, and cool in a refrigerator until just beginning to set. Meanwhile garnish the trout and the well of the plate with lemon, capers and dill.

13. When the aspic has become syrupy and slightly thickened, spoon it carefully over the fish fillets. Place the serving plate and chill for 1-2 hours, or until set.

TIME: Preparation takes 45 minutes to 1 hour. Total cooking time is about 50 minutes plus at least 1 hour to chill the dish.

HERRINGS WITH APPLES

The addition of apples beautifully complements the delicious and wholesome flavour of herring.

SERVES 4

2 large dessert apples
1 large onion
4 large potatoes, peeled and sliced
Salt and freshly ground black pepper
140ml/¼ pint dry cider
4 herrings, cleaned
60g/2oz dried breadcrumbs
60g/2oz polyunsaturated margarine
1 tbsp fresh chopped parsley

1. Peel, quarter, core and slice one of the apples. Peel and slice the onion thinly.

2. Lightly grease a shallow baking dish and layer with the apple, potatoes and onions, seasoning well with salt and pepper between layers.

3. Pour the cider over the potato layers and cover the dish with foil. Bake in an oven preheated to 180°C/350°F/Gas Mark 4, for 40 minutes.

4. Meanwhile, prepare the fish. Cut the heads and tails from the herrings and split them open from the underside.

5. Put the herrings, belly side down, on a flat surface and carefully press along the back of each fish with the palms of your hands, pushing the backbone downwards.

6. Turn the herrings over and with a sharp knife, carefully prise away the backbone, pulling out any loose bones as you go. Do not cut the fish into separate fillets. Wash and dry them well.

7. When the potato layers are cooked, remove the dish from the oven and arrange the herring fillets over the top.

8. Sprinkle the breadcrumbs over the herrings and dot with half of the margarine.

9. Increase the oven temperature to 200°C/400°F/Gas Mark 6 and return the dish to the oven for about 10-15 minutes, or until the herrings are cooked and brown.

10. Core the remaining apple and slice into rounds, leaving the skin on.

11. Melt the remaining margarine in a frying pan and gently sauté the apple slices.

12. Remove the herrings from the oven and garnish with the apple slices and the chopped parsley. Serve at once.

TIME: Preparation takes 15-20 minutes, cooking takes about 50 minutes.

VARIATION: Use small mackerel instead of herrings in this recipe.

SERVING IDEAS: Serve with a carrot, orange and watercress salad.

TANDOORI FISH

A firm-fleshed white fish is ideal for this dish; it is not necessary to use an expensive fish. The fish should be handled carefully as most white fish tend to flake during cooking.

SERVES 4

460g/1lb fillet or steak of any white fish
½ tsp salt
5mm/¼-inch cube of root ginger, peeled and coarsely chopped
2 cloves garlic, coarsely chopped
1 tsp ground cumin
1 tsp ground coriander
½ tsp garam masala
¼-½ tsp chilli powder
¼ tsp Tandoori colour or a few drops of red food colouring mixed with 1 tbsp tomato purée
Juice of ½ lemon
3 tbsps water
2 tbsps cooking oil

Mix the following ingredients in a small bowl
2 heaped tbsps flour
½ tsp chilli powder
¼ tsp salt

1. Wash the fish and dry on kitchen paper. Cut into 2.5cm/1-inch squares. If using frozen fish, defrost it thoroughly first.

2. Add the salt to the ginger and garlic and crush to a smooth pulp.

3. In a small bowl, mix together the ginger/garlic pulp, cumin, coriander, garam masala, chilli powder and Tandoori colour or tomato purée mix. Add the lemon juice and water and mix thoroughly. Keep aside.

4. Heat the oil over a medium heat in a non-stock or cast iron frying pan. Dust each piece of fish in the seasoned flour and put in the hot oil in a single layer, leaving plenty of room in the pan.

5. Fry for 2½ minutes on each side, and drain on kitchen paper. Now return all the fish to the pan.

6. Hold a sieve over the pan and pour the spice liquid mixture into it. Press with the back of a metal spoon until the mixture in the sieve looks dry and very coarse; discard this mixture.

7. Stir gently and cook over medium heat until the fish is fully coated with the spices and the liquid dries up. Remove from the heat and serve.

TIME: Preparation takes 15 minutes, cooking takes 15-20 minutes.

SERVING IDEAS: Serve garnished with shredded lettuce leaves, sliced cucumber and raw onion rings.

GRILLED TUNA WITH ROSEMARY

A quick and easy way of serving sumptuous fresh tuna steaks.

SERVES 4

2 large tuna steaks
2 tbsps olive oil
1 tbsp chopped parsley
1 tsp chopped rosemary
1 clove garlic, finely chopped
2 tbsps breadcrumbs
Salt and pepper
2 lemons

1. Cut out the bone from each tuna steak.

2. Brush the steaks on one side with a little of the oil and sprinkle over half of the parsley, rosemary, garlic, breadcrumbs and salt and pepper.

3. Preheat a cast iron griddle or a heavy-based frying pan. When the griddle or frying pan is really hot, wipe over a little oil with a piece of kitchen paper and place on the tuna steaks, herbed side down.

4. Quickly brush the tops of the steaks with the remaining oil and sprinkle over the remaining parsley, rosemary, garlic, breadcrumbs and a little salt and pepper. Turn the steaks to cook other side.

5. Cook the tuna for 8-12 minutes or to your liking. If using a griddle, give the steaks a quarter turn on each side to give them a charred grid pattern.

6. Serve immediately, accompanied with lemon halves.

TIME: Preparation takes about 10 minutes and cooking takes about 8-12 minutes, depending on how well cooked you like your fish.

SERVING IDEA: Serve with a tossed green salad.

COOK'S TIP: If the steaks are very thick, mark them on each side on the hot griddle and then transfer to a hot oven to finish cooking.

STUFFED SALMON TROUT

SERVES 6-8

1 fresh whole salmon trout, weighing
　　1.25kg/2½lbs, cleaned
900g/2lbs fresh spinach
1 small onion
60g/2oz polyunsaturated margarine
60g/2oz walnuts, roughly chopped
20g/4oz fresh white breadcrumbs
1 tbsp fresh chopped parsley
1 tbsp fresh chopped thyme
¼ tsp grated nutmeg
Salt and freshly ground black pepper
Juice of 2 lemons
Watercress and lemon slices, to garnish

1. Carefully cut the underside of the fish from the end of the slit made when the fish was cleaned, to the tip of the tail.

2. Place belly side down, on a work surface, spreading the cut underside out.

3. Press down along the backbone of the fish, pushing the spine downwards towards the work surface.

4. Turn the fish over and using a sharp knife, carefully pull the backbone away from the flesh, cutting it out with scissors at the base of the head and tail.

5. Pull out any loose bones with tweezers. Lay the fish in the centre of a large square of lightly oiled foil and set aside.

6. Wash the spinach leaves well and tear off any coarse stalks. Put the spinach into a large saucepan and sprinkle with salt. Do not add any extra water. Cover and cook over a moderate heat for about 3 minutes.

7. Turn the spinach into a colander and drain well, pressing with the back of a wooden spoon to remove all the excess moisture, then chop very finely using a sharp knife.

8. Chop the onion finely and sauté gently in about 15g/½oz of the margarine until soft, but not coloured.

9. Stir the onion into the spinach along with the walnuts, breadcrumbs, herbs, nutmeg, salt, pepper and half of the lemon juice. Mix well to blend evenly.

10. Push the stuffing firmly into the cavity of the trout, re-shaping the fish as you do so.

11. Seal the foil over the top of the fish, but do not wrap it too tightly. Place the fish in a roasting tin and bake in an oven preheated to 180°C/350°F/Gas Mark 4, for 35 minutes.

12. Carefully unwrap the fish and transfer it to a large serving dish. Using a sharp knife, peel away the skin from all exposed sides of the fish and from the underside if possible.

13. While the fish is still hot, dot with the remaining margarine, sprinkle with the remaining lemon juice, then serve garnished with the watercress and lemon.

TIME: Preparation takes 35-40 minutes, cooking takes about 40 minutes.

COOK'S TIP: If you feel that you cannot bone the fish yourself, ask your fishmonger to do it for you, but explain that you wish the bone to be removed from the underside of the fish.

CHICKEN STUFFED PEPPERS

Using chicken to stuff peppers makes a lower cholesterol meal than using minced beef. If wished, serve the peppers for a first course in which case the recipe will feed 6.

SERVES 3

3 large green or red peppers

60ml/4 tbsp olive oil

1 small onion, finely chopped

1 stick celery, finely chopped

1 clove garlic, crushed

2 chicken breasts, skinned, boned and diced

2 tsps chopped parsley

½ loaf of stale French bread, made into crumbs

1-2 eggs, beaten

Salt and pepper

90g/6 tsps dry breadcrumbs

1. Cut the peppers in half lengthwise and remove the cores and seeds. Leave the stems attached, if wished.

2. Melt the oil in a frying pan and add the onion, celery, garlic and chicken. Cook over a moderate heat until the vegetables are softened and the chicken is cooked. Add the parsley. Season with salt and pepper.

3. Stir in the French breadcrumbs and add enough beaten egg to make the mixture hold together.

4. Spoon the filling into each pepper half, mounding the top slightly. Place the peppers in a baking dish that holds them tightly packed.

5. Pour enough water down the inside of the dish to come about 1.25cm/½-inch up the sides of the peppers. Cover and bake in an oven preheated to 180°C/350°F/Gas Mark 4, for about 45 minutes, or until the peppers are just tender.

6. Sprinkle each with the dried breadcrumbs and place under a preheated grill until golden brown.

TIME: Preparation takes about 30 minutes and cooking takes about 45-50 minutes.

VARIATION: Use spring onions in place of the small onion. Add chopped nuts or black olives to the filling, if wished.

CHICKEN WITH 'BURNT' PEPPERS AND CORIANDER

'Burning' peppers is a technique for removing the skins which also imparts a delicious flavour to this favourite vegetable.

SERVES 4

---

2 red peppers, halved
1 green pepper, halved
60ml/4 tbsps vegetable oil, for brushing
1 tbsp olive oil
2 tsps paprika
¼ tsp ground cumin
Pinch cayenne pepper
2 cloves garlic, crushed
450g/1lb canned tomatoes, drained and chopped
3 tbsps fresh chopped coriander
3 tbsps fresh chopped parsley
Salt, for seasoning
4 large chicken breasts, boned
1 large onion, sliced
60g/2oz flaked almonds

---

1. Put the peppers, cut side down, on a flat surface and gently press them with the palm of your hand to flatten them out.

2. Brush the skin side with 2 tbsps of the vegetable oil and cook them under a hot grill until the skin chars and splits.

3. Wrap the peppers in a clean towel for 10 minutes to cool.

4. Unwrap the peppers and carefully peel off the charred skin. Chop the pepper flesh into thin strips.

5. Heat the olive oil in a frying pan and gently fry the paprika, cumin, cayenne pepper and garlic for 2 minutes, stirring to prevent the garlic from browning.

6. Stir in the tomatoes, coriander, parsley and season with a little salt. Simmer for 15-20 minutes, or until thick. Set aside.

7. Meanwhile, heat the remaining vegetable oil in a casserole and sauté the chicken breasts, turning them frequently until they are golden brown on both sides.

8. Remove the chicken and set aside. Gently fry the onions in the oil for about 5 minutes, or until softened but not overcooked.

9. Return the chicken to the casserole with the onions and pour on about 280ml/½ pint of water. Bring to the boil.

10. Cover the casserole and simmer for about 30 minutes, turning the chicken occasionally to prevent it from burning.

11. Remove the chicken from the casserole and boil the remaining liquid rapidly to reduce to about 90ml/3 fl oz of stock.

12. Add the peppers and the tomato sauce to the chicken stock and stir well.

13. Return the chicken to the casserole, cover and simmer very gently for another 30 minutes, or until the chicken is tender.

14. Arrange the chicken on a serving dish with a little of the sauce spooned over. Sprinkle with flaked almonds and serve any remaining sauce separately.

SHANGHAI NOODLES

*In general, noodles are more popular in northern and eastern China, where
wheat is grown, than in other parts of the country. Noodles make a popular snack
in Chinese tea houses.*

SERVES 4

3 tbsps oil
340g/12oz chicken breast, thinly sliced
175g/6oz Chinese leaves
6 spring onions
2 tbsps soy sauce
Freshly ground black pepper
Dash sesame oil
460g/1lb thick Shanghai noodles

1. Heat the oil in a wok and add the
chicken strips. Stir-fry for 2-3 minutes.

2. Meanwhile, cook the noodles in boiling,
salted water until just tender – about 6-8
minutes. Drain in a colander and rinse
under hot water. Toss in the colander to
drain and leave to dry.

3. Stack up the Chinese leaves and, using a
sharp knife, cut across into thin strips.
Thinly slice the spring onions.

4. Add the shredded Chinese leaves and
spring onions to the chicken in the wok
along with the soy sauce, pepper and
sesame oil. Cook for about 2 minutes and
toss in the cooked noodles. Stir well and
heat through. Serve immediately.

TIME: Preparation takes about 10 minutes, cooking takes 6-8 minutes.

VARIATION: Add shredded fresh spinach, and sliced mushrooms, and cook
with the Chinese leaves.

BUYING GUIDE: Shanghai noodles are round fresh egg noodles, thicker
than spaghetti. They are available in Chinese supermarkets and also some
delicatessens. If unavailable, substitute dried Chinese noodles.

CHICKEN WITH BLACKCURRANT SAUCE

The sharp tang of blackcurrants makes an ideal partner for lightly cooked chicken.

SERVES 4

---

4 chicken breasts, boned and skinned
2 tbsps sesame oil
225g/8oz fresh blackcurrants
Juice of 1 orange
140ml/¼ pint red wine
Sugar to taste
Orange slices and fresh blackcurrants, to garnish

---

1. Season the chicken breasts with a little salt. Heat the oil in a shallow frying pan.

2. Gently sauté the chicken breasts for 7-8 minutes on each side until they are golden brown and tender.

3. Top and tail the blackcurrants and put them into a small pan, along with the orange juice and red wine. Bring to the boil, then cover and simmer gently until the blackcurrants are soft.

4. Using a liquidiser or food processor, blend the blackcurrants and the cooking juice for 30 seconds.

5. Rub the blended purée through a fine nylon sieve with the back of a wooden spoon, pressing the fruit through to reserve all the juice and pulp but leaving the pips in the sieve.

6. Put the sieved purée into a small saucepan and heat gently, stirring constantly until the liquid has reduced and the sauce is thick and smooth.

7. Arrange the chicken breasts on a serving dish, and spoon the blackcurrant sauce over. Garnish with orange slices and fresh blackcurrants.

TIME: Preparation takes 15 minutes, cooking takes about 15 minutes.

PREPARATION: To test if the chicken breasts are cooked, insert a skewer into the thickest part, then press gently – if the juices run clear the meat is cooked.

VARIATION: Use blackberries instead of blackcurrants in this recipe.

SERVING IDEAS: Serve with a selection of fresh green vegetables.

POUSSINS ESPAGNOLE

The olive oil in this recipe gives a wonderful flavour to the sauce without loading it with saturated fat.

SERVES 4

4 small poussins
Salt and freshly ground black pepper
Olive oil
4 small wedges of lime or lemon
4 bay leaves
1 small onion, thinly sliced
1 clove garlic, crushed
460g/1lb tomatoes
140ml/¼ pint red wine
140ml/¼ pint chicken or vegetable stock
1 tbsp tomato purée
1 green chilli, seeded and thinly sliced
1 small red pepper, cut into thin strips
1 small green pepper, cut into thin strips
2 tbsps chopped blanched almonds
1 tbsp pine nuts
12 small black olives, pitted
1 tbsp raisins

1. Rub the poussins inside and out with salt and pepper. Brush the skins with olive oil and push a wedge of lime or lemon, and a bay leaf into the cavity of each one.

2. Roast the poussins, uncovered, in an oven preheated to 190°C/375°F/Gas Mark 5, for 45 minutes or until just tender.

3. Meanwhile, heat 2 tbsps olive oil in a large frying pan and gently sauté the onion and the garlic until soft, but not coloured.

4. Cut a slit in the skin of each tomato and plunge into boiling water for 30 seconds.

5. Using a sharp knife carefully peel away the skins from the blanched tomatoes.

6. Chop the tomatoes roughly, discarding the seeds and cores.

7. Add the chopped tomatoes to the cooked onion and garlic and sauté gently for a further 2 minutes.

8. Add all the remaining ingredients and simmer for 10-15 minutes, or until the tomatoes have completely softened and the sauce has thickened slightly.

9. Arrange the poussins on a serving dish and spoon a little of the sauce over each one. Serve the remaining sauce in a jug.

TIME: Preparation takes 20 minutes, cooking takes about 45 minutes.

SERVING IDEAS: Serve with rice and a mixed green salad.

COOK'S TIP: If the poussins start to get too brown during cooking, cover them with foil.

CHICKEN PALAK

Chicken Palak is a delicious combination of chicken and spinach with fennel, coriander and chillies.

SERVES 4-6

1kg/2.2lbs chicken quarters, skinned
3 tbsps vegetable oil
2 medium-sized onions, finely chopped
2.5cm/1-inch cube of root ginger, peeled
   and finely grated
2-3 cloves garlic, crushed

Make a paste of the following 4 ingredients by adding 3 tbsps water

1 tsp ground turmeric
1 tsp ground fennel
1 tsp ground coriander
½ tsp chilli powder

1½ tsps salt or to taste
90ml/3 fl oz warm water
1 heaped tbsp polyunsaturated margarine
1-2 cloves garlic, finely chopped
6-8 curry leaves
½ tsp cumin seeds
½ tsp fennel seeds
1-2 dried red chillies, coarsely chopped
460g/1lb fresh or 225g/8oz frozen leaf
   spinach, (defrosted and drained),
   coarsely chopped
60ml/4 tbsps natural yogurt
½ tsp garam masala

1. Cut each chicken quarter in half, separating leg from thigh and cutting each breast into two, lengthwise.

2. Heat the oil over a medium heat and sauté the onions, ginger and garlic for 6-8 minutes until the onions are lightly browned.

3. Adjust heat to low, add the spice paste and stir and cook for 4-5 minutes. Rinse out the bowl with 2 tbsps water and add to the spice mixture. Stir and cook for a further 2-3 minutes.

4. Add the chicken, stir and sauté over a medium-high heat for 3-4 minutes, or until it changes colour. Add 1 tsp of the salt and the warm water, bring to the boil, cover the pan and simmer for 15 minutes, stirring occasionally.

5. In a separate pan, melt the margarine over a medium heat and add garlic and curry leaves followed by the cumin, fennel and red chillies, stirring briskly.

6. If using fresh spinach, wash thoroughly and remove any hard stalks. Add the spinach and the remaining salt to the spices, stir and cook for 5-6 minutes then mix into the chicken. Bring to the boil, cover the pan and simmer for 20 minutes, stirring occasionally.

7. Mix the yogurt and garam masala together and beat until the yogurt is smooth. Add to the pan, stir and mix thoroughly. Cook uncovered for 6-8 minutes over a medium heat, stirring frequently.

TIME: Preparation takes 25-30 minutes, cooking takes about 1 hour.
SERVING IDEAS: Serve with brown rice and Spicy Mushrooms.

CHICKEN CHAAT

Recipes do not have to be elaborate to be tasty, and Chicken Chaat is a perfect example. Cubes of chicken meat, stir-fried with a light coating of spices look impressive with a colourful salad.

SERVES 4

680g/1½lbs chicken breast, skinned and boned
1 tsp salt or to taste
2-3 cloves garlic, coarsely chopped
2 tbsps vegetable oil
1½ tsps ground coriander
¼ tsp ground turmeric
¼-½ tsp chilli powder
1½ tbsps lemon juice
2 tbsps finely chopped coriander leaves

1. Wash the chicken and dry on kitchen paper. Cut into 2.5cm/1-inch cubes.

2. Add the salt to the garlic and crush to a smooth pulp.

3. Heat the oil in a non-stick or cast iron frying pan, over a medium heat.

4. Add the garlic and sauté until it is lightly browned.

5. Add the chicken and sauté for 6-7 minutes, stirring constantly.

6. Add the ground coriander, turmeric and chilli powder. Fry for 3-4 minutes, stirring frequently. Remove from the heat as soon as the chicken is cooked through, and stir in the lemon juice and coriander leaves.

TIME: Preparation takes 15 minutes, cooking takes 12-15 minutes.

SERVING IDEA: Serve with a Carrot Pilau, naan bread and salad.

SWEET AND SOUR TURKEY MEATBALLS

These easy-to-prepare turkey meatballs are served with a highly flavoured sweet and sour sauce.

SERVES 4

1 small onion, finely chopped

2 tbsps olive oil

460g/1lb raw turkey

1 clove garlic, crushed

2 tbsps fresh parsley, chopped

2 tbsps blanched almonds, finely chopped

Freshly ground black pepper

¼ tsp mixed spice

1 tbsp chopped raisins

2 tbsps fresh wholemeal breadcrumbs

1 egg, beaten

4 spring onions, thinly sliced

280ml/½ pint pure tomato juice

2 tbsps tomato purée

Juice of ½ lemon

1 tbsp honey

1 green chilli, seeded and finely chopped

2 slices fresh pineapple, finely chopped

1 medium red pepper, cut into thin strips

2 carrots, peeled and coarsely grated

1. Sauté the onion gently in the olive oil until just transparent.

2. Using a food processor or mincer, finely chop or mince the raw turkey.

3. Put the minced turkey into a large bowl, along with the garlic, parsley, almonds, pepper, mixed spice, raisins, breadcrumbs and egg.

4. Stir in the cooked onion and the oil, mixing well to combine all ingredients thoroughly.

5. Divide the mixture into 16 and shape each piece into a small ball. Chill for 30 minutes.

6. Put all the remaining ingredients into a shallow pan and bring to the boil. Cover the pan and simmer the sauce gently for 10 minutes, stirring occasionally.

7. Carefully drop the chilled meatballs into the sauce. Re-cover and simmer for a further 20 minutes, or until the meatballs are completely cooked.

TIME: Preparation takes 20-25 minutes, plus 30 minutes chilling. Coooking takes about 35 minutes.

PREPARATION: If the sauce evaporates too quickly, add a little stock or water to keep it to a thin enough consistency.

SERVING IDEA: Serve with brown rice or wholemeal pasta.

OLIVE-STUFFED RABBIT MEAT

This impressive dish comprises saddle of rabbit with an olive stuffing cooked in a tomato-based sauce.

SERVES 4

2 saddles of rabbit
½ tsp chopped rosemary
Salt and pepper
3 tbsps chopped olives
1 clove garlic, chopped
2 tbsps olive oil
3 large tomatoes, skinned, seeded and
    chopped
120ml/4 fl oz chicken stock
120ml/4 fl oz tomato juice

1. Remove the bones from the 2 saddles, taking care not to pierce the meat.

2. Sprinkle the inside of the meat with the rosemary and salt and pepper.

3. Mix together the chopped olives and the garlic. Spread this stuffing down the centre of each saddle.

4. Roll up the meat, taking care to roll tightly and neatly.

5. Secure the 2 rolls of stuffed meat with thin kitchen string.

6. Heat the olive oil in a frying pan, add the meat and cook briskly to seal the rolls until golden brown on all sides.

7. Add the tomatoes, stock and tomato juice to the pan, stirring well to mix.

8. Season with salt and pepper, cover and cook on a moderate heat for 20 minutes. Check the level of the liquid in the pan frequently, stirring and shaking the ingredients from time to time.

9. After 20 minutes, remove the rolls to a hot plate and allow the remaining sauce to reduce and thicken.

10. Cut the rolls into slices and serve on the tomato sauce.

TIME: Preparation takes about 30 minutes and cooking takes about 45 minutes.

VARIATION: For the stuffing, use a mixture of green and black olives, or just green olives.

WATCHPOINT: Boning the saddle is a delicate job. The meat should not have any holes at all, but should you make a small hole, patch it with a piece of meat.

HERBED POTATO BAKE

Potatoes, layered with onions and herbs and baked until crisp on top make a delicious side dish.

SERVES 4

4 medium potatoes, peeled and sliced
    thickly
3 medium onions, sliced
120ml/4 fl oz chicken stock
1 tbsp chopped fresh marjoram
Salt and pepper
Polyunsaturated margarine

1. Layer the potatoes and onions in a lightly oiled ovenproof dish. Pour the stock in down the side of the dish.

2. Sprinkle with the marjoram, salt and pepper and dot with a little margarine.

3. Bake in an oven preheated to 180°C/350°F/Gas Mark 4, for 40 minutes or until the potatoes are tender. If necessary, brown under a preheated grill.

TIME: Preparation takes 15 minutes and cooking takes 40 minutes.

VARIATION: Use other fresh herbs, such as basil, chives, tarragon or dill.

Broad Beans Provencal

Fresh broad beans mixed with herbs and tomatoes taste delicious.

SERVES 4

460g/1lb fresh or frozen broad beans
30g/1oz polyunsaturated margarine
2 tsps Herbes de Provence
4 tomatoes, skinned, seeded and diced
Salt and pepper

1. Cook the broad beans in boiling, salted water for about 8 minutes or until tender.

2. Drain and refresh under cold water. Peel off outer skin of the beans if wished.

3. Melt the margarine and toss with the broad beans and Herbes de Provence.

4. Heat through and add the tomatoes, salt and pepper. Serve immediately.

TIME: Preparation takes 5 minutes and cooking takes 8 minutes.

PREPARATION: If the beans are young and tender there is no need to remove the outer skins.

SPICY MUSHROOMS

The use of mushrooms is somewhat limited in Indian cooking. However, in the West the abundant supply of mushrooms throughout the year makes it possible to create mouthwatering dishes at any time.

SERVES 4

340g/12oz button mushrooms
2 tbsps vegetable oil
2-3 cloves garlic, crushed
½ tsp salt or to taste
½ tsp chilli powder
2 tbsps finely chopped fresh coriander
    leaves
1 tbsp lemon juice
2 tbsps besan (gram flour or chick pea
    flour), sieved

1. Wash the mushrooms and chop them coarsely.

2. Heat the oil over a medium heat and add the garlic. Allow the garlic to turn slightly brown, add the mushrooms and stir and cook for 2 minutes.

3. Add salt, chilli powder and coriander leaves; stir and cook for 1 minute.

4. Add the lemon juice and mix well.

5. Sprinkle the besan over the mushroom mixture, stir and mix immediately. Remove from the heat.

TIME: Preparation takes 15 minutes, cooking takes 6-8 minutes.

SERVING IDEAS: Serve with Chicken Palak.

COLCANNON

*This traditional Irish dish of potatoes, cabbage and onion is a wonderful
combination and makes a change from ordinary mashed potatoes.*

SERVES 4

90g/3oz finely chopped onion, leek or
    spring onions
30g/1oz polyunsaturated margarine
60ml/2 fl oz skimmed milk
460g/1lb cooked potatoes, mashed
225g/8oz cooked cabbage

1. Melt the margarine in a pan, add the onion, leek or spring onions and gently sauté until soft.

2. Add the milk and the well-mashed potatoes and stir until heated through.

3. Chop the cabbage finely and beat into the mixture over a low heat until all the mixture is pale green and fluffy.

TIME: Preparation takes 30 minutes, including cooking the vegetables.
Cooking takes 10 minutes.

CARROT PILAU

An imaginative way to turn plain boiled rice, left over or freshly cooked, into a colourful and tasty pilau which can be served with meat, fish or chicken curry.

SERVES 4-6

275g/10oz basmati rice, washed and soaked in cold water for 30 minutes
520ml/18 fl oz water
1 tsp salt or to taste
Vegetable oil
1 tsp cumin or caraway seeds
1 medium onion, finely sliced
2 cinnamon sticks, broken up
4 green cardamom pods, split open at the top
1 tsp garam masala or ground mixed spice
175g/6oz coarsely grated carrots
120g/4oz frozen garden peas
½ tsp salt or to taste

1. Drain the rice thoroughly and put into a saucepan with the water.

2. Bring to the boil, stir in the salt and 1 tsp oil.

3. Allow to boil steadily for 1 minute.

4. Place the lid on the saucepan and simmer for 12-15 minutes. Do not lift the lid during this time.

5. Remove the pan from heat and keep it covered for a further 10 minutes.

6. Meanwhile, prepare the rest of the ingredients.

7. Heat 2 tbsps oil in a large pan or frying pan over a medium heat and fry the cumin or caraway seeds until they pop.

8. Add the onion, cinnamon and cardamom. Sauté for 4-5 minutes, until the onions are lightly browned, stirring frequently.

9. Add the garam masala or ground mixed spice, stir and cook for 30 seconds.

10. Add the carrots, peas and the salt; stir and cook for 1-2 minutes.

11. Now add the rice and stir and mix gently using a metal spoon or fork. Remove the pan from the heat and serve.

TIME: Preparation takes 10-15 minutes plus time needed to soak the rice, cooking takes 25-30 minutes.

COOK'S TIP: When the rice is cooked use a metal spoon or fork to stir it as a wooden or plastic one will squash the tender grains.

FRUIT PLATE

This attractive medley of fruit can be varied to suit your taste and makes a refreshing dessert that can be served after a filling main course.

SERVES 4

1 green fig
2 kiwi fruit
2 fresh dates
1 guava
1 paw paw
120g/4oz lychees
½ small pineapple
1 fresh mango
120g/4oz seedless grapes
½ small melon
225g/8oz watermelon
2 tbsps orange juice
2 tbsps lemon juice
60g/2oz chopped walnuts, or pine nuts
   (optional)

1. Select a large, shallow serving platter on which to arrange the fruit.

2. Cut the fig into quarters lengthways and arrange on a plate.

3. Peel the kiwi fruits, slice the fruit thinly and arrange alongside the fig, reserving a few slices for the watermelon.

4. Cut the dates in half lengthways and remove the stones. Place the dates on the serving plate.

5. Cut the guava in half and slice into wedges with a sharp knife. Peel the paw paw and slice this into thin crescents.

Arrange the guava slices and paw paw alternately onto the plate along with the other prepared fruit.

6. Peel the lychees and remove the stones from the stalk end using the rounded tip of a swivel potato peeler. Discard the stones and place the fruit on the serving platter.

7. Peel the pineapple and cut away any brown eyes which may remain in the flesh. Cut the pineapple into slices and remove the core using a sharp knife or apple corer. Cut the slices into small wedges and arrange on the plate.

8. Peel the mango and cut the flesh into slices, discarding the stone.

9. Halve the grapes. Place the mango and grapes in an alternate pattern, alongside the rest of the fruit on the serving plate.

10. Cut the melon in half and remove the seeds. Slice the melon flesh into small wedges then cut off the skin.

11. Cut the watermelon and cut into similar sized wedges, without removing the pips or skin. Arrange the melon wedges on either side of the plate and decorate with the remaining kiwi fruit.

12. Mix together the orange and lemon juice and chopped nuts, then sprinkle evenly over the fruit on the plate. Cover with cling film and chill well before serving.

TIME: Preparation takes about 30 minutes, plus chilling time.

PREPARATION: Canned lychees could be used in place of the fresh fruit in this recipe, as could canned pineapples, kiwis and mangoes, but make sure they are packed in natural juice which should be drained before serving.

RHUBARB SORBET

This very refreshing sorbet makes an ideal light dessert after a rich or spicy meal.

SERVES 4

460g/1lb rhubarb
340ml/12 fl oz water
175g/6oz sugar

1. Peel the rhubarb and cut the stalks into short pieces.

2. Put into a saucepan and mix together with the water and sugar. Bring to the boil, then reduce the heat and cook for 5 minutes.

3. Blend until smooth using a hand mixer or liquidiser and pour into a shallow container. Freeze for 2 hours or until just beginning to set.

4. Break up the partially frozen ice using a fork or electric whisk, then return to the container and continue to freeze for another hour.

5. Break up the ice crystals again, mashing it well. Pour into a container, cover and freeze until completely solid.

TIME: Preparation takes about 10 minutes and freezing takes 5-6 hours.

SERVING IDEAS: Serve on a bed of finely sliced rhubarb which has been cooked for 2 minutes in very little water and sweetened to your liking. Allow the sorbet to soften somewhat before serving.

SPICED ORANGES WITH HONEY AND MINT

An unusual combination of flavours blend to create this light and very refreshing dessert.

SERVES 4

280ml/½ pint clear honey
420ml/¾ pint water
2 large sprigs of fresh mint
12 whole cloves
4 large oranges
4 small sprigs of mint, to decorate

1. Put the honey and the water into a heavy-based saucepan. Add the mint and cloves and slowly bring to the boil.

2. Stir the mixture to dissolve the honey and boil rapidly for 5 minutes, or until the liquid is very syrupy.

3. Cool the mixture completely, then strain the syrup through a nylon sieve into a jug or bowl to remove the sprigs of mint and cloves.

4. Using a potato peeler, carefully pare the rind very thinly from one of the oranges, including as little of the white pith as possible.

5. Cut the pared orange rind into very fine shreds with a sharp knife.

6. Put the shreds of peel into a small bowl and cover with boiling water. Allow to stand until cold then drain completely, reserving only the strips of peel.

7. Stir the strips of peel into the honey syrup and chill well.

8. Peel all the oranges completely, cutting off all the skin and white pith using a sharp knife.

9. Slice the oranges into thin rounds and arrange on four individual serving plates.

10. Pour the chilled syrup over the oranges on the plates and garnish with the small sprigs of mint just before serving.

TIME: Preparation takes 20 minutes, cooking takes about 5 minutes.

PREPARATION: It is important that all the white pith is removed from the oranges, otherwise this will give a bitter flavour to the dessert.

VARIATION: Use ruby grapefruits in place of the oranges in this recipe. Allow half a grapefruit per person and cut it into segments rather than slices to serve.

Strawberry Sorbet

This makes the ideal dessert for summer when strawberries are plentiful and cheap.

SERVES 4

1 medium lemon
280ml/½ pint water
175g/6oz sugar
680g/1½lbs strawberries
2 egg whites

1. Pare the lemon rind from the lemon and put into the water with the sugar.

2. Heat slowly until the sugar has dissolved then boil for 5 minutes.

3. Strain and set aside to cool.

4. Hull the strawberries reserving a few for decoration. Purée the remainder in a food processor or liquidiser then pass through a fine nylon sieve to remove the seeds. Add the juice of half the lemon.

5. Whisk the egg whites until very stiff, then carefully, but thoroughly, fold into the purée. Combine all the ingredients well.

6. Put into a shallow tray and place in the freezer.

7. Remove when half frozen, beat well and return to the freezer. When half frozen again, beat well and turn into an airtight container. Freeze until solid.

8. Place in the refrigerator about 15 minutes before serving.

9. Serve in wine glasses topped with the whole berries.

TIME: Preparation takes 20 minutes, cooking takes 5 minutes. Freezing takes about 8 hours.

COOK'S TIP: It is better to leave the sorbet in the freezer overnight at the end of Step 7.

GREEN GRAPE SHORTCAKE

Plenty of fibre in the diet will help to reduce the amount of cholesterol found in the blood, and the wholemeal flour and grape skins in this recipe are a good source of fibre.

SERVES 6

60g/2oz polyunsaturated margarine
30g/1oz soft brown sugar
60g/2oz wholemeal flour
30g/1oz ground almonds
225g/8oz green grapes, halved and pitted
570ml/1 pint water
Thinly pared rind of 2 lemons
1 tbsp honey
15g/½oz powdered gelatine
Few drops yellow food colouring (optional)

---

1. Put the margarine, sugar, flour and almonds into a large bowl.

2. Work the margarine into the dry ingredients using your fingertips, pressing the mixture together gently to form a soft dough.

3. Knead the dough lightly until it is smooth.

4. Line the base of a 20cm/8-inch loose-bottomed cake tin with silicone paper. Press the shortcake dough evenly over the base of the lined tin, making sure that it is pushed well into the sides.

5. Bake in an oven preheated to 190°C/375°F/Gas Mark 5, for 15 minutes or until the shortcake is firm and golden brown. Remove from the oven and allow to cool in the tin.

6. Lightly grease the inside of the cake tin above the shortcake with a little vegetable oil.

7. Arrange the grape halves on top of the shortcake.

8. Put the water and lemon rind into a small pan and bring to the boil. Allow to simmer for 5 minutes, then remove the pan from the heat and allow the liquid to cool completely.

9. Strain the lemon liquid through a nylon sieve to remove the rind. Measure off 420ml/¾ pint of the strained liquid and stir in the honey.

10. Put the remaining lemon liquid into a small saucepan and heat gently until it is very hot, but not boiling.

11. Sprinkle over the gelatine and allow to stand until it has completely dissolved.

12. At this stage the food colouring can be added to the liquid if wished.

13. Stir the gelatine mixture into the lemon and honey mixture and stand in a cool place until it is beginning to set.

14. Spoon the partially set jelly carefully over the grapes making sure that they remain evenly spread.

15. Stand the shortcake in a refrigerator until the jelly has set completely. Serve in wedges.

TIME: Preparation takes 45 minutes, plus cooling and chilling. Cooking takes about 20 minutes.

PREPARATION: It is important never to boil gelatine or it will not set properly.

APPLE SORBET WITH BRANDY AND SULTANAS

Sorbets make an ideal dessert for anyone on a low-fat diet. Try this unusual combination for a real change of flavours.

SERVES 4-6

570ml/1 pint apple juice
60g/2oz caster sugar
45g/1½oz packet of dried apple flakes
120g/4oz sultanas
140ml/¼ pint brandy
Few drops green food colouring (optional)
1 egg white

---

1. Put the apple juice in a heavy-based saucepan along with the sugar. Heat gently, stirring until the sugar has dissolved. Bring the apple juice to the boil and boil quickly for 5 minutes. Remove from the heat and cool completely.

2. Put the apple flakes into a bowl along with the sultanas and brandy. Add enough of the apple syrup to cover the mixture, then allow to soak for 4 hours.

3. Mix the apple flakes, sultanas and brandy together to form a pulp, adding the green colouring at this stage if required.

4. Whisk the apple pulp into the remaining syrup, mixing thoroughly to blend evenly.

5. Pour the apple mixture into a shallow container and freeze for 2 hours or until just beginning to set.

6. Break up the partially frozen ice using a fork or electric whisk, then return to the freezer tray and continue to freeze for another hour.

7. Break up the ice crystals again, but this time mash thoroughly until they form a thick slush.

8. Whisk the egg white until it is stiff, then quickly fold into the ice slush. Return to the freezer tray and freeze until completely solid.

9. Allow the ice to soften for 15 minutes before spooning into individual glass dishes.

TIME: Preparation takes 10 minutes, plus 4 hours soaking and 5-6 hours freezing time.

COOK'S TIP: Use 280ml/½ pint of apple purée in place of the apple flakes and reduce the amount of apple juice used to 420ml/¾ pint.

VARIATION: Omit the brandy from this recipe and replace with more apple juice.

APPLE SPICE RING

This delicious cake is also a healthy cake as it contains plenty of fibre and little fat.

460g/1lb dessert apples, cored
90g/3oz ground hazelnuts
120g/4oz wholemeal flour
30g/1oz bran
60g/2oz light muscovado sugar
1½ tsps baking powder
1 tsp ground cinnamon
Pinch ground nutmeg
Pinch ground cardamom
30g/1oz polyunsaturated margarine, melted
120ml/8 tbsps skimmed milk
Dessert apple slices and icing sugar, to
    decorate

1. Grate the apples, with their skin on, on the coarse side of a grater. Place in a mixing bowl along with the hazelnuts.

2. Stir in the flour, bran, sugar, baking powder and spices. Mix to blend well.

3. Add the melted margarine and beat until it is evenly blended. Stir in the milk and mix to a stiff batter.

4. Carefully spoon into a greased 20.5cm/8 inch ring tin and level the top. Bake in an oven preheated to 180°C/350°F/Gas Mark 4, for 45 minutes or until a skewer inserted into the centre of the cake comes out clean.

5. Allow to cool slightly in the tin then transfer to a wire rack to cool. Dust with icing sugar and decorate with apple slices dipped in lemon juice, just before serving.

TIME: Preparation takes about 15 minutes, cooking time is about 45 minutes.

SERVING IDEAS: Serve hot as a dessert with apple purée.

COOK'S TIP: If you do not have a ring tin, place an empty jam jar in the centre of a 20.5cm/8-inch deep sided cake tin.

VARIATION: Use almonds instead of hazelnuts in this recipe.

PEARS IN RED WINE

A delicious way of serving whole fresh pears, this dessert looks especially impressive served in glass dishes.

SERVES 6

570ml/1 pint dry red wine
1 strip lemon peel
Juice of ½ lemon
225g/8oz sugar
1 small piece cinnamon stick
6 pears, ripe but firm
15g/½oz flaked almonds

1. Put the wine, lemon peel and juice, sugar and cinnamon into a large deep saucepan and bring to the boil, stirring until the sugar dissolves. Allow to boil rapidly for 1 minute.

2. Carefully peel the pears lengthways and remove the small eye from the base of each pear. Leave the stalks intact.

3. Place the peeled pears upright in the boiled wine mixture. Return the pan to the heat, bring to the boil, then simmer very gently for 20 minutes, or until the pears are soft but not mushy.

4. Allow the pears to cool in the syrup until lukewarm, then remove and arrange in a serving dish.

5. Strain the syrup through a nylon sieve to remove the lemon peel and spices.

6. Return the syrup to the saucepan and boil rapidly until it becomes thicker and syrupy.

7. Cool the syrup completely before spooning it carefully over the pears in the serving dish. Before serving, sprinkle with the flaked almonds.

TIME: Preparation takes 25 minutes, cooking takes 30 minutes.

PREPARATION: If the syrup does not completely cover the pears in the saucepan, allow them to cook on their side, but make sure they are turned frequently and basted to ensure an even colour.

VARIATION: Use white wine in place of the red wine in this recipe.

FROZEN ORANGES

A tasty and attractive sorbet that is served in orange 'shells'.

SERVES 4

About 6 oranges to make 280ml/10 fl oz
    orange juice
140ml/¼ pint water
150g/5oz sugar

1. Cut the tops off the oranges and remove the pulp with the help of a small spoon, keeping the orange skins whole.

2. Squeeze the juice from the pulp and measure it until you have 280ml/10 fl oz of freshly squeezed juice – you may require more oranges for this.

3. Mix the orange juice, together with the water and sugar. Mix well with a whisk and then pour into a shallow container and freeze for 2 hours, or until just beginning to set.

4. Break up the partially frozen ice using a fork or electric whisk, then return to the container and continue to freeze for another hour.

5. Break up the ice crystals again, mashing well. Pour into the container and freeze until solid.

6. Before serving, remove the mixture from the freezer and allow to soften slightly in the refrigerator. Spoon into the orange 'shells' and serve.

TIME: Preparation takes about 30 minutes and freezing takes 5-6 hours.

SERVING IDEA: Serve with crystallized orange peel.

COOK'S TIP: When you have removed the pulp from the oranges, place the skins in the freezer, so that they are very cold when you fill them with the sorbet.

FRUIT TRUFFLES

*These delicious little nibbles get all the sweetness they require from fresh bananas
without the need for cream or sugar.*

MAKES 10

2 bananas
Juice of ½ orange
Finely grated rind 1 orange
150g/5oz ground almonds
30g/1oz blanched almonds
1 tbsp cocoa powder

1. Chop the bananas into a large bowl and using a potato masher, mash them until they are smooth.

2. Mix in the orange juice and rind.

3. Stir in the ground almonds, mixing well to blend evenly. Place the mixture in a refrigerator and chill for about 30 minutes.

4. Using a sharp knife, finely chop the blanched almonds into small pieces.

5. Mix the chopped almonds into the cocoa powder, and place on a flat plate.

6. Remove the banana mixture from the refrigerator and divide into 10 portions.

7. Roll each portion into a small ball, dusting your hands lightly with a little icing sugar.

8. Roll each ball into the cocoa and almond mixture pressing gently. Roll each one evenly to give a good coating. Place in small paper cases and chill once again.

TIME: Preparation takes about 25 minutes, plus chilling time.

COOK'S TIP: Do not keep these delicious sweets for long after they have been made, or the banana will go brown and wet.

VARIATION: Use walnuts in place of almonds in this recipe.

Index

Apple Sorbet with Brandy and
Sultanas 102

Apple Spice Ring 104

Black-Eyed Bean and Orange
Salad 42

Broad Beans Provençal 84

Butter Bean, Lemon and Fennel
Salad 22

Carrot Pilau 90

Celery and Apple Soup 8

Chicken Chaat 76

Chicken Palak 74

Chicken Stuffed Peppers 64

Chicken with Blackcurrant Sauce 70

Chicken with 'Burnt' Peppers and
Coriander 66

Chickpea Salad 28

Chinese Salad 20

Cod Curry 48

Colcannon 88

Frozen Oranges 108

Fruit Plate 92

Fruit Truffles 110

Green Grape Shortcake 100

Grilled Fish 50

Grilled Tuna with Rosemary 60

Herbed Potato Bake 82

Herrings with Apples 56

Lentil and Vegetable Curry 34

Mixed Pepper Salad 32

Mushroom Pasta Salad 38

Noodles with Ginger and Oyster
Sauce 26

Olive-Stuffed Rabbit Meat 80

Orange, Grapefruit and Mint
Salad 36

Paella 52

Pears in Red Wine 106

Penne with Spicy Chilli Sauce 24

Poussins Espagnole 72

Rhubarb Sorbet 94

Shanghai Noodles 68

Singapore Fish 46

Smoked Mackerel Pâté 12

Spaghetti Marinara 44

Spiced Oranges with Honey and
Mint 96

Spicy Mushrooms 86

Spicy Vegetable Fritters 14

Stir-Fry Pasta Salad 40

Strawberry Sorbet 98

Stuffed Salmon Trout 62

Summer Pasta Salad 18

Sweet and Sour Turkey Meatballs 78

Tandoori Fish 58

Tomato and Pepper Ice 16

Trout in Aspic 54

Vegetable Stew with Herb
Dumplings 30

Vichyssoise 10